SUCCESS JOURNAL

Judge Mlambo

authorHOUSE®

AuthorHouse™ UK Ltd.
1663 Liberty Drive
Bloomington, IN 47403 USA
www.authorhouse.co.uk
Phone: 0800.197.4150

Published by AuthorHouse   04/16/2014

ISBN: 978-1-4969-7780-9 (sc)
ISBN: 978-1-4969-7781-6 (e)

About the Book Interior: During the last hundred years, the publishing houses have printed millions different books about how to achieve success. Why then have I had the temerity to write another book about "How" to achieve success? And after I have written it, why should you bother to read it?

Fair questions, both; and are answered in this book.

"Compared to what we ought to be," said the famous Professor William James of Harvard, "compared to what we ought to be, we are only half-awake. We are making use of only a small part of our physical and mental resources. Stating the thing broadly, the human individual thus lives far within his limits. He possesses powers of various sorts which he habitually fails to use."

Those powers which you "habitually fail to use!" The sole purpose of this book is to help you discover, develop and profit by those dormant and unused assets.

"Education," said Dr John G. Hibben, former President of Princetown University, "education is the ability to meet life's situations." If by the time you have finished reading this book—if you aren't then a little better equipped to meet life's situations, then you shall consider this book to be the total failure, so far as you are concerned. For "the great aim of education," said Herbert Spencer "is not knowledge but action."

- And this is an action book, your life personal journal on "How to" achieve what you want in life.
- Success leaves clues and those clues are contained in this book.
- You will find that the "How" part of success it's easy to achieve if your "Why" is clear.
- Easy is anything that can be done and you must be willing to pay the price.
- So let's go. Let's get down to brass tacks at once.

Success Life Journal

1

. . . .

Vision—Success Life Journey

The A B C   D E F Success Journey

There is no such thing as standing still. If you are not going 'forward' you are actually going 'backwards'. The shortest distance between two points is a straight line represented by A (this is where you Are now) and B (this is where you want to Be). Your plan is the tiny steps you are going to take to reach you goals however be aware that the Costly Curves lure you to other things (Have) that is why there are obstacles along those paths to instruct you and not to obstruct you. More importantly, do not get caught in the Dead tracks of Fear.

Fear of failing.
Fear of the unknown.
Fear of rejection.
Fear of success.

The opposite to fear is Faith which gives you Enthusiasm to continue. There is one very important quality that you need in order to build your vision and that is COURAGE, and there are 4 words that make up the word Courage and they are:

1. Desire
2. Commitment
3. Belief
4. Action

"If you don't know where you are going, you will probably end up somewhere else." You need a strong burning Desire for your vision. You must be totally Committed to it and have the Faith or Belief to put that commitment into Action. Doubt is the biggest killer between commitment and action. Remember; always have awareness of your belief (faith) to conquer any doubt.

2

. . . .

Why and How to use Your Journal

Every journey begins with a single step and ends with a single step.

Whether you want a healthier, better-looking body, improve your financial status, enhance your relationships or achieve any of your other dreams there is always a gap between where you are now and where you want to be. Bridging that gap requires jus three simple things: Planning, Focus and Action.

Putting pen to paper offers you an effective way to figure things out, keep you focused and inspire you into action. There is almost something quite magical that happens when you write down your objectives or dilemmas. It is as though, in the mere act of writing down what they are, you start finding ways to succeed or overcome them.

The fact that you are writing about them instead of mental manifestation, creates a different space between you and the objective or dilemma. It is within this space that strategies and solutions are born and have room to mature. Writing things down helps you clarify exactly what needs to be done or solved. When we describe things only in our minds our wild imaginations tend to feed us distorted or exaggerated information about things are, positively or negatively. Whatever we continuously focus on, we tend to attract, like metal filing to a magnet. Focussing on unimportant things creates confusion, stress and worry. Worrying is as useful as a rocking chair; it gives you something to do but takes you nowhere. When we describe our objectives or dilemmas in writing, we click into a more precise, more specific and a much more realistic mode.

Then, as we reread what we have written, we create a new mental picture to replace the exaggerated or distorted ones we have been 'toiling' with. Now herein lies the real magic. Once we finally see things as they actually are instead of as we think they are, we can then start to see an actual path of accomplishment or solvability.

It takes 21 days to break a habit and 21 days to make something a habit i.e. you break an old habit by replacing it with a new habit for a minimum of 21 days.

Use your journal to capture who you are and what you stand for. Assess where you are, find out where you are going, set and achieve your goals, solve dilemmas, figure out life and plan each day before it plans you.

Also use it to write down your thoughts, ideas, feelings, quotes, and humour. Once you have formed your daily planning habit, form another golden habit by going 21 days mental fast. Yes, starve yourself of negative television, radio, newspapers and magazines for next

21 days and replace that input with positive wisdom quotes and tips.

Becoming a more effective thinker on paper is a proven way of becoming a more effective and balance person in practice.

3

. . . .

Values

Who I am and what I stand for. One of the simplest ways to conclude this exercise is to break down your life into the various roles that you play or would like to play and then add the pertinent values to them, i.e. :

Father = disciplined, strict, fair, loving, providing

Daughter = charming, forgiving, patient, kind

Brother = protective, sharing, unselfish, cultured

Friend = trust, loyal, honest, unconditional

Colleague = integrity, respect, humour, serve

TICK YOUR TOP APPROPRIATE VALUES BELOW

Accountability	Good IQ	Social
Activities	Help	Trust
Analytical	Honesty	Truthfulness
Caring	Hope	Uncompromising
Charming	Humble	Vision
Cleanliness	Independent	Vocabulary

Communication	Integrity	Watchful
Compassion	Intellectual Growth	Wealth
Competent	Joyful	Welcoming
Competitive	Justice	Wellness
Contribute	Kindness	Wilful
Creative	Leadership	Wisdom
Cultured	Leave A Legacy	Wonderful
Curiosity	Liberality	Yearning
Debt free	Love	Zealous
Decisiveness	Make A Difference	Other:
Detail	Merit	
Determination	Moderation	
Discipline	Motivational	
Diversity	Numbers	
Dynamic	Order	
Education	Organisation	
Empathy	Organised	
Energetic	Originality	
Enthusiastic	Participation	
Fair	Passion	
Faith	Patience	
Faithful	Peace	
Family	People	
Feelings	Persistent	
Financial Independent	Places	
Fit and Healthy (example)	Popular	
Forgiveness	Pride	

Judge Mlambo

Friendly	Proficiency
Friendship	Quietness
Fulfilment	Recreation
Fun	Reputation
Fun-Loving	Respect
Generosity	Responsibility
God Honouring	Service To Others

4

. . . .

My Philosophy

Once you have identified what your top values are write a statement about what each value means to you.

Value: **Statement:**

Fit and Healthy   I exercise daily and eat the right
                     kinds of food in moderation

5

. . . .

10 Main Reasons Why People Don't Achieve Their Goals

1. DON'T HAVE ANY—The main reason why people do not achieve their goals is because they do not have any. There is big difference between goals and desires. A goal is something you write it down; it is a statement that is specific, well formulated and clear to understand with a deadline. Studies around the world have shown that in classes of 100 students who were exposed to the Power in Planning, only 3 took the time and effort to do this and put it into action. The astonishing observation after 20-year period showed that the 3% were happier, more satisfied and had accumulated more wealth than the 97% of the remaining students combined; the remaining 97% of students only had desires for their career goals. The Oxford Dictionary definition of 'desire' is a strong feeling of wanting to have something or wishing for something to happen.

2. FEAR OF FAILURE—Most people had goals once but they failed to achieve them, so they gave up. Once bitten twice shy. What these people do not realise is that obstacles come to instruct and not to obstruct. You only fail if you give up. Often not achieving your goal the first time is the best lesson if you are prepared to learn from your mistakes. Thomas Edison was asked once what it felt like to fail 5,000 times. He answered by saying "I found 5,000 ways how not to make a light bulb."

3. WRONG REASONS—People set goals that they don't really deep down inside want. It sound like it would be great because they hear someone else wish for it, or they are trying to achieve the goal for someone else and not themselves. In the film 'Dead Poets Society', the young scholar sadly committed suicide because of the pressure from the goal his father wanted him to succeed at. You need to find your own passion and purpose, and take responsibility for your own life.

4. UNREALISTIC AND IMPOSSIBLE MYTHS—If you can conceive it and believe it, you can achieve it. A great number of people give up before they start as they set goals that they do not believe are possible to achieve, or they seem unrealistic. Many people broke the 4 minute mile that same year Roger Bannister made the impossible, possible.

5. LACK OF VISION—People does not achieve their goals—not because their goals are too big but because they are too small. If you have a small goal, your mind thinks . . . . "If I achieve it or not, it doesn't matter . . . ." When the goal is too small you are not able to enflame the imagination. You must be excited and enthusiastic about it and its only large goals that do that. The birds were mocking the snail for crawling up the cherry tree in winter. "There are no cherries in winter", they laughed. The snail replied, "But there will be when I get there." Now that's vision! Make decisions that are bold and courageous for your life. After all, this is YOUR LIFE—have great goals that excite and enthuse your imagination—goals that have juice!

6. DON'T USE THEIR SUBCONCIOUS MIND TO THEIR ADVANTAGE—Many people don't know how to use their subconscious mind to their advantage, or worse don't know it exists. The great inventors like Alexander Bell, Albert Einstein, Thomas Edison etc all said they did not get the ideas from themselves. The ideas came from beyond our conscious mind. We are a little piece of the hologram of the whole universe. If you don't feel it is because that part of you that is holographic is your subconscious mind. A better name for your subconscious mind is your "Beyond Mind". This second mind that we have inside us is a tiny piece of the universe. It is all omnipresent. The Oxford Dictionary defines 'subconscious' as an adjective of or concerning the part of the mind of which one is not fully aware but which influences one's actions and feelings.

7. LACK OF FAITH AND CONFINDENCE—People lack faith and confidence even though we hear a lot about faith. For example, there is a biblical statement that says . . . "If you have faith the size of a mustard seed you can move mountains . . . ." Christ and apostles were in a boat on a lake when the storm was raging. He began walking on the water and Peter decided to do the same but when he realise what he was, he sank. Christ looked at him and said, "Oh ye of little faith, why do ye doubt?" Learn to relax in faith and confidence and things will start to happen which you thought were not possible.

8. STUCK IN A COMFORT ZONE—Too many people dislike change. They are stuck in a comfort zone, in a rut waiting for something to happen. The height of insanity is doing the same thing and expecting a different result. Without big, clear, specific goals with deadlines it's like trying to sail the high seas without a sail. You will end up where you don't want to be. When you set goals correctly, you set your sail, but you still have to put the action in and do the sailing by prioritising your important goals in order to utilise the best investment of your time. Don't wait for things to happen, make things happen.

9. VALUES AND GOALS OUT OF ALIGNMENT— Another reason why few who had set goals still didn't achieve them is that they were not aligned with who they are and what they with stand for. For example, people who do not agree with nicotine, alcohol, or other drug related products should not work for, or support, tobacco, liquor or pharmaceutical type companies, etc. Create your own personal philosophy in order of priority.

10. PRIORITIES OUT OF BALANCE-Many of us are caught up in the frenzy of consumerism, where the primary focus is on money and often lack of it. Our careers and professions have become money driven instead of purpose and passion driven. And we justify this by telling ourselves that once we have put in all the time and effort we will then have the time and money to spend with our families and loved ones!!!

You see there is not enough time to accomplish everything that comes our way on a daily basis. But there is always enough time to do the important things. Like most people, you probably started every year off with exciting new year resolutions – only to find they fall by the wayside before the first month is over. Why not start this year off differently; knowing who you are, what you stand for and what you really want to accomplish. In the same way as you realign your personal and family life, you can realign your social, career and financial goals. "Thoughts are things." The size of your goals is directly proportional to the size of your thoughts.

The key to a happy, successful life is living a balance lifestyle. You life goals must be divided into eight categories.

1. Financial and wealth goals
2. Professional and career goals
3. Intellectual and educational goals
4. Physical and health goals
5. Recreational and social goals
6. Communicational and cultural goals
7. Spiritual and emotional goals
8. Family and home goals

For each category you must have your philosophy, assess your philosophy for each, have a plan for each category and have action plan for each category.

6

. . . .

Goal Setting Workshop

Where you were 5 years ago and where are you now?

If you started working at age 20, and hope to retire at young age of 60, that would mean a total of 480 productive months: 40 years x 12 months = 480 productive months. Now work out for yourself how many months you have left before you retire at 60. For example: If you're 37 years old today, you're left with: 60-37 = 23 years x 12 months =276 productive months and 275 next month and so on.

WORKSHOP

1. LIST 5 THINGS YOU ALREADY ACCOMPLISHED THAT YOU ARE APROUD OF.

1.
2.
3.
4.
5.

Take credit for yourself before working on your future.

2. WHAT DO YOU WANT IN NEXT 10 YEARS? LIST 50 THINGS ONE UNDER THE OTHER.

Notes: not what you think you can get but what you want. Let your imagination and creative power run wild, let it flow.

1.
2.
3.
4.
5.
6.
7.
8.
9.
10.
11.
12.
13.
14.
15.
16.

17.
18.
19.
20.
21.
22.
23.
24.
25.
26.
27.
28.
29.
30.
31.
32.
33.
34.
35.
36.
37.
38.
39.
40.
41.
42.
43.
44.
45.
46.
47.

48.

49.

50.

Note: you can continue this list.

3. **GIVE EACH ITEM A NUMBER, WHAT YOU THINK IT WILL TAKE TO ACHIEVE IT. 1, 3, 5, 10+ YEARS.**

4. **COUNT HOW MANY 1, 3, 5, 10+**

Notes:—When you have accomplished some goals you need more goals to accomplish.

- It is important that when you reach a goal that is significant to you, to celebrate.

- Family goals celebrate with the family; it helps each member of the family to have a longer list of goals.

- Goals to replace other goals, be all you possible can.

- Remember celebration creates excitement

5. ON LIST OF 1 YEAR GOALS PICKUP 4 MOST IMPORTANT.

Notes:—What got you turned on? What excite you about life?

- And what got you turned off about life?

6. WHY ARE THOSE 4 GOALS IMPORTANT TO YOU?

Notes:—When the why gets stronger the how gets easier.

- Without strong why, the how seems impossible.

- Why, what for is good questions because the purpose is more important than the object or things.

- Some goals should be personal development because it is not what you get that make you valuable but what you become. E.g. "here is why I want . . . ."

7. WHAT KIND OF PERSON MUST I BECOME TO ACHIEVE ALL I WANT?

Notes:—This is the time for the truth. Do you need to be wise? Do you need a coach?

- Do you need to be healthy? Do you need a spiritual coach?

- When you knock on the door, will the opportunity open the door for you? Will it let you come in?

- Put everything on the list form your head to paper. Don't trust your memory.

- If it is not important take it off from your list, rearrange and change your list.

- Two words on inequity that you should learn, one is positive the other is negative: Behold and Beware

- Behold = opportunities, possibilities, the future changes, the next person you meet.

- Be a major contributor in life of others.

- To married people—if the parents are ok, the kids are ok, personal development is the best investment for your family.

- Take care of yourself for me and I will take care myself for you. e.g. in an aeroplane, in case of emergency principle.

- Negative = Beware

- Beware of what you become in pursuit of what you want.

- Don't be so obsessed with something that you compromise yourself and your values.e.g. Judas story in the bible. H e was unhappy with himself after he got the money.

- Take care yourself first, accept the pain not the guilt.

7

....

My Balanced Lifestyle Questionnaire

How do you rate yourself out of 100, mildly agree, agree and strongly agree. Choose a number between 10-100 that best describe you.

1. I have a detailed investment and retirement plan.

2. I enjoy my career as it is in line with who I am and what I stand for.

3. I stretch my brain through regular, concentrated, imaginative and creative exercises.

4. I eat a balanced diet of fresh carbohydrates, protein and fats three times per day and drink at least eight glasses of water.

5. I pursue exciting and fulfilling hobbies or sporting activities regularly.

6. I take time to listen and attend art and theatre functions.

7. I have a written personal constitution that clarifies who I am and what I stand for and why I am here.

8. I have a written family mission statement that we all adhere to, including eating meals at the dining room table.

9. I live within my means and have a good credit rating.

10. I am an asset to my company, industry and I am willing to help others.

11. I read different books regularly from novels, business to self development.

12. I maintain my ideal body weight and shape by exercising at least three times per week above my normal physical activity.

13. I take at least one holiday for a minimum of two weeks each year.

14. I respect and get along with different people from different backgrounds.

15. I don't bottle up my feelings and emotions. I express them freely, easily and often.

16. I have written specific family goals that we all participate in at least once a year.

17. I save regularly and have at least six month's income saved.

18. I pay for and attend courses each year in order to advance in my chosen career, industry and company.

19. I keep up with current technology trends and advancements both in and out of my field.

20. I have an annual dental and medical check up.

21. I leave my work at work and home at home.

22. I control my temper and I am seldom angry.

23. I love to help others with a generous heart without wanting anything in return.

24. I spend one—on-one time regularly with each member of my family.

25. My earnings have increased significantly over the past five years.

26. I set aside regular time for research, study and learning.

27. I am willing to work on activities over and above my job description and I am always looking for ways to improve my company's bottom line.

28. I detoxify my body at least once per annum and do not consume harmful and addictive substances e.g. alcohol, nicotine or other drugs.

29. I regularly meet with people outside of the work place.

30. I often volunteer for community projects.

31. I have strong spiritual beliefs which reflect my daily thoughts, actions and commitment.

32. I respect and embrace other's space, goals, views and differences with grace and quickly forgive and forget any disagreement.

33. I stay abreast and research financial and wealth matters myself, especially after receiving any advice.

34. I don't waste time and energy on corporate politics.

35. I filter out as much negative information as possible by not listening to trivial news both the media and when I am socialising.

36. I get sufficient sleep and I am generally happy, strong and full of energy.

37. I travel often and meet new and interesting people and forge lasting friendships.

38. I have a good sense of humour and exercise good posture and body language.

39. I study and attend spiritual gatherings/ meetings regularly.

40. I seek advice regularly on efficient tax matters and update my will and testament accordingly.

8

Balanced Living Score Calculations

FINANCIAL/ WEALTH	PROFESSIONAL/ CARREER	INTELLECTUAL/ EDUCATIONAL	PHYSICAL/ HEALTH
1 =	2 =	3 =	4 =
9 =	10 =	11 =	12 =
17 =	18 =	19 =	20 =
25 =	26 =	27 =	28 =
33 =	34 =	35 =	36 =
Total divide by 5=	Total divide by 5=	Total divide by 5=	Total divide by 5=
Average%	Average%	Average %	Average%

RECREATIONAL/ SOCIAL	COMMUNICATIONAL/ CULTURAL	SPIRITUAL/ EMOTIONAL	FAMILY/ HOME
5 =	6 =	7 =	8 =
13 =	14 =	15 =	16 =
21 =	22 =	23 =	24 =
29 =	30 =	31 =	32 =
37 =	38 =	39 =	40 =
Total divide by 5=	Total divide by 5=	Total divide by 5=	Total divide by 5=
Average %	Average %	Average %	Average %

Transfer the percentages that you have scored to the wheel on the next page to the appropriate area of life. Join the percentages of all the areas of life together to see how balanced your wheel life is and in what areas you need to spend more time and improve.

1. In which area of your life did you score the highest percentage? What does this tell you about your priorities?

   Answer:

2. Which areas do you want to invest more time and resources in? how will you or others benefit from this investment in time?

   Answer:

9

Life Cycle

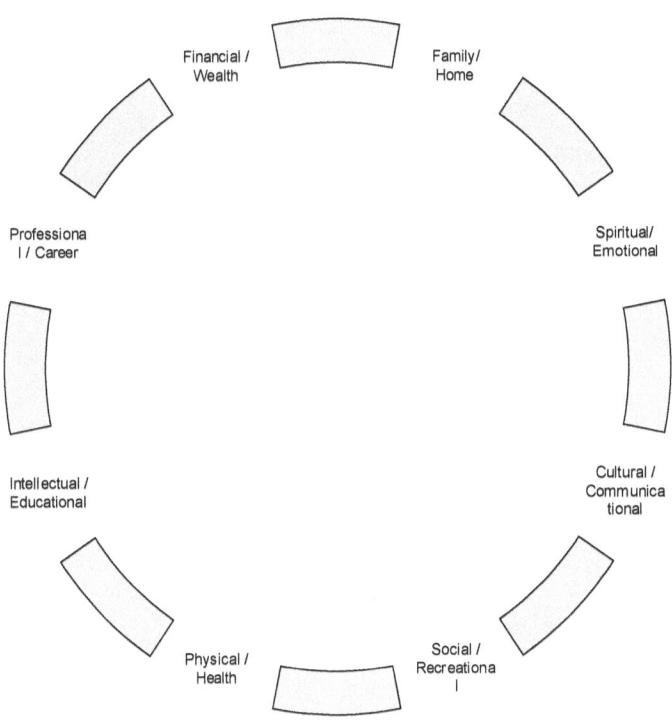

Financial /
Wealth

Family/
Home

Professiona
l / Career

Spiritual/
Emotional

Intellectual /
Educational

Cultural /
Communica
tional

Physical /
Health

Social /
Recreationa
l

Judge Mlambo

If there was a simple step-by-step formula to help me get what you want out of life would I take a closer look?

What is my no. 1 priority?
Answer:

Why did I pick that one?
Answer:

Why is that important to me?
Answer:

What will happen if I don't achieve it?
Answer:

Why would that concern me?
Answer:

10

My Vision Statement

This is what I want to BE, DO and HAVE.

_____

_____

_____

_____

_____

_____

_____

_____

_____

_____

_____

_____

_____

_____

_____

_____

_____

11

My Mission Statement

This is HOW I am going to ATTAIN it.

_____

_____

_____

_____

_____

_____

_____

_____

_____

_____

_____

_____

_____

_____

_____

_____

12

· ·

Take Stock of your Financial Goals

INCOME STATEMENT

INCOME

Salary: R
Interest: R
Dividend: R
Real Estate:
Cash Flow:
R
R
Businesses
Cash Flow:
R
R

PASSIVE INCOME =
(Interest+ Dividends+ Real
Estate + Business Cash Flow)

TOTAL INCOME:
R

Number of Children:
Per Child Expense: R

EXPENSES
Taxes: R
Home Mortgage: R
School Loan Payment: R
Car Payment: R
Credit Card Payment: R
Retail Payment: R
Bank Loan Payment: R
Other Expenses: R
Child Expenses: R

TOTAL EXPENSES:
R

BALANCE SHEET

ASSETS

Savings: R

Stocks/ Unit trusts/ Cash   No. of shares

Deposits

Cost/Share

R

R

Real Estate:

Deposit:

Cost

R

R

R

Business:

Deposit:

Cost

R

R

R

LIABILITIES

Home Mortgage: R

Real Estate Mortgage: R

School Loans: R

Car Loan: R

Credit Card Loan: R

Retail Debt: R

Liability: (Business) R

Bank Loan: R

13

Monthly Income and Expenditure Schedule

INCOME	JAN	FEB	MAR	APR	MAY	JUN	JUL	AUG	SEP	OCT	NOV	DEC
Salary												
Other Income												
(Less : Pay Yourself First)												
TOTAL GROSS INCOME												
EXPENSES												
Business / Events												
Clothing												
Domestic												
Donations												
Entertainment												
Groceries												
Holidays												
Insurance												
Investment / Life Assurance												
Medical Aid (Private)												
Other												

Fuel / Parking												
Rent / Mortgage												
School Fees												
Security												
Self-development												
Stationery												
Taxes / UIF												
Telephone / Mobile / Internet												
Vehicle Instalment 1												
Vehicle Instalment 2												
Vehicle Maintenance												
Water and Electricity												
TOTAL EXPENSES												
(INCOME MINUS EXPENSES) NETT INCOME												
CUMULATIVE												

14

. . . .

Ideas, Thoughts, Imaginations

_____

_____

_____

_____

_____

_____

_____

_____

_____

_____

_____

_____

_____

_____

_____

_____

_____

15

. . . .

What Do I Want to Accomplish in next 10 Years and Why?

What do I want to accomplish in the next 10 years?	Years	WHY?	Prioritise 1, 2, 3

Once you have answered 'why' for each thing, separate your list into 3 categories:

Short term (1-3 years), medium term (3-5yers) and long term (5-10).

16

Balance Living— My 3 Main Short, Medium And Long Term Goals

FINANCIAL / WEALTH	PROFESSIONAL / CARRER	COMMUNICATION / CULTURAL	SPIRITUAL / EMOTIONAL
SHORT TERM	SHORT TERM	SHORT TERM	SHORT TERM
MEDIUM TERM	MEDIUM TERM	MEDIUM TERM	MEDIUM TERM
LONG TERM	LONG TERM	LONG TERM	LONG TERM

RECREATIONAL / SOCIAL	INTELLECTUAL / EDUCATIONAL	PHYSICAL / HEALTH	FAMILY / HOME
SHORT TERM	SHORT TERM	SHORT TERM	SHORT TERM
MEDIUM TERM	MEDIUM TERM	MEDIUM TERM	MEDIUM TERM
LONG TERM	LONG TERM	LONG TERM	LONG TERM

17

Things I Have Already Accomplished

Write down all the things that you have already accomplished and you are proud of.

Then write what they meant to you and how they made you feel.

Things I have already accomplished	What they meant and how they made me feel

18

My Top 10 Goals In Order
of Importance

Prioritise the top ten items from your **10 Year and
short, medium and long term goal lists** through a
process of importance. Then, next to each item, write
down the reason for wanting it or the benefit in attaining
it and by what date.

Goals —Wants	State the Benefits —Why? What for?	Short, Medium or Long term	By When?	Area of Life
1.				
2.				
3.				
4.				
5.				
6.				
7.				
8.				
9.				
10.				

19

Visualisation—My Dream Collage

Collect and paste pictures of everything you want to be, do or have. There is also a separate space to paste pictures of each of your top ten dreams on the Goal Planning Sheets.

20

The Person I Must Become

Describe the person you must become to accomplish your goals and how you are going to get there?

_____

_____

_____

_____

_____

_____

_____

_____

_____

_____

_____

_____

_____

_____

_____

_____

_____

21

. . . .

Affirmations to Support My Goals

An affirmation is a declaration that you believe is true, which is often said repeatedly to yourself from past experiences. Unfortunately they are often used negatively. For example: if you repeatedly say, "I hate Mondays", you will always hate Mondays. Affirmations should always contains the 3 P's: **P**ronoun '**I** ', **P**resent tense and **P**ositive.

e.g.	I am financial independent	Finance

22

Personal Development

List the things that will enable you to grow: i.e. the books you should read, the seminars you should attend, skills you will need, people you should meet, the place you should visit, etc.

_____

_____

_____

_____

_____

_____

_____

_____

_____

_____

_____

_____

_____

_____

23

. . . .

Achieving Your Lifelong Objectives

1. Establish in order of priority an unshakable philosophy of good character, generosity, love, trust, integrity, loyalty, faith, honesty, etc. This will ease your decision-making when confronted at various crossroads along your interesting journey of life. **REMEMBER:** obstacles are there to instruct and not obstruct.

2. Take the responsibility to achieve. Decide who you really want to become (be), put into action now (do) and then you will achieve (have). **REMEMBER:** aim for goals that are bigger than you.

3. Break your intermediate objectives into smaller achievable steps. **REMEMBER:** climb any mountain one step at a time.

4. Commit daily to your detailed planned deadlines. **REMEMBER** how breakfast is made. The hen was involved in producing the egg, but the pig was committed to producing the bacon.

5. Develop good daily habits and they will make you. Learn to take control of your daily activities, instead of letting them control you. **REMEMBER**, if you are not doing that which is bringing you closer to your

goals on a daily basis, you are wasting your time and potentially wasting your life.

6. Feed the mind—keep motivated and maintain a positive attitude on a daily basis. Feed your mind with positive material by reading good books and listening to motivational and inspirational audio recordings. Attend self development courses, industry-related seminars and training programmes. **REMEMBER,** if you don't feed your mind with positive thoughts, negative thoughts will grow.

7. Feed your body—keep in good physical shape. High energy and strength are required to achieve your life goals. Have your own exercise and eating programme. Drink 8 to 10 glasses of water a day and get lots of good uninterrupted sleep. **REMEMBER** to avoid harmful addictions such as alcohol or other drugs.

8. Feed your soul—keep in good spiritual shape. Read and study spiritually everyday. **REMEMBER:** For what profit is it to a man if he gains the whole world, and loses his own soul? Or what will a man give in exchange for his soul?

9. Grow continuously—the only thing that is constant is change. Change is inevitable. Accept, adjust and adapt. **REMEMBER,** there is no such thing as standing still. If you are not going forward, you are actually going backwards.

10. Make a difference—live with passion and purpose, **REMEMBER,** find a need and fill it.

24

PLANNING and PREPARATION
for SUCCESS

10 Positive Rules to Turn Desires into Accomplishments

1. Write down all the things and conditions you earnestly desire and prioritise them in order of importance. Place no limitations on your desires. As you grow and develop, your values change, therefore your desires change. So change your list daily by adding or taking out from it.

2. Create a mental prototype in your mind of the exact things or conditions your desire from your list. e.g. it is not enough to say "I want a big holiday house", Be definite about the things and conditions by asking why? What for?

3. Determine exactly what you intend to give in return for the things and conditions you desire. There is no such as "something for nothing."

4. Set a definite date when you intend to get the conditions and things you desire.

5. Create a definite plan for is plan carrying out your

desires. Begin at once, whether you are ready or not to put this plan into action.

6. Write out a clear, concise statement of all the conditions and things you desire and the time limit for their attainment. State what you intend to give in return for the desires and describe clearly the plan through which you intend to get them.

7. Read your written statement aloud three times each day: morning, midday and night. As you read, visualise and feel and believe yourself already in possession of your desires.

8. Think of what you want as often as possible, but do not talk to anyone about you plan except God within you, which will unfold to your conscious mind the method of accomplishment. If you talk to people about it your Universal Power is leaking away, as electricity does in what we call a "ground"—earth leakage.

9. Ask yourself all the time: "what is the best possible use of my time right now?" If you are not doing that which is bringing you closer to your desires, you are wasting your time and therefore you are wasting your life.

10. Do not be jealous or resent conditions or things other people have. It will have same "earth leakage". Instead, help as many people as possible to accomplish their desires.

25

The Serenity Prayer

God grant me the serenity
to accept the things I cannot change;
courage to change the things I can;
and wisdom to know the difference.
Living each day at a time;
Enjoying one moment at a time;
Accepting hardships as the pathway to peace;
Taking, as He did, this sinful world
as it is, not as I would have it;
Trusting that He will make all things right
if I surrender to His Will;
That I may be reasonable happy in this life
and supremely happy with Him
Forever in the next
AMEN
By Reinhold Niebuhr

26

COMMITMENT

A chicken and a pig were having a brief discussion. The chicken said to the pig, "I am committed to giving one egg every single day."

"That's not a commitment," the pig said. "That's involvement. Giving bacon; that's a commitment!"

I _____

Residing at _____

_____ *personally commit to spending 15 hours developing my philosophy and finding out who I am, what I stand for and what I want to be, do and have. I will set specific written short, medium and long term goals with deadlines in all eight areas of my life and continuously strive to live a Balanced Lifestyle.*

I will consistently spend 15 to 20 minutes formally planning each day. Then I will list each activity in order of priority, distinguishing the 'urgent' from 'important' and spend my time more effectively and efficiently with the emphasis on attitude and persistent action. I will evaluate where I am every week.

Judge Mlambo

I will read and / or listen to different literature on self development everyday. I will strive daily to make a positive difference, living each day with passion and purpose.

Signature _____

Date_____

27

. . . .

If You Believe It, You Can Achieve It!

Now, we've all heard this before, but how many of us actually apply this concept? Don't let other people destroy your dreams and tell you what you can't do. The most successful people in the world where they are today, because they believed that anything was possible, and that they could literally change the world if they wanted to. And so can you!

Here's where positive thinking comes into the picture. Over the years, your brain has been trained to think in a certain way and to expect certain outcomes. You need to change that perception, so your brain will start to anticipate better, more positive and even truly amazing outcomes. If you believe in yourself and expect good things to happen, there's no reason why you can't achieve your dreams. Here are a few motivational exercises you can do:

- Talk to yourself in the mirror. It sounds strange, but no one can give you a better pep talk than you. Tell yourself who you are and what you plan to achieve.

- Define your vision and write it down. Then look at this piece of paper everyday to remind yourself of what you want and where you're going.

- Don't listen to other people's negativity. It can be extremely destructive.

- Stop using the word "I can't" keep telling yourself you can, until you believe it.

Follow your heart and do what you love. It is actually possible to make a career out of something that you are passionate about. It may require you to take a risk, go back and study again, work harder than anyone else, be creative or do some serious research, but it is possible. You just need to believe it!

How did the world's top achievers become so successful?

The answer is simply this: they believed that they could achieve anything they put their minds to. They did not limit their dreams. Instead, they decided what they wanted and they worked really hard, took risks, studied further, defied adversity and, basically, did whatever they needed to do to get where they are today.